Let's Read About Pets

# Parakeets

by JoAnn Early Macken

Reading consultant: Susan Nations, M.Ed., author/literacy coach/consultant

WEEKLY WR READER®
EARLY LEARNING LIBRARY

Please visit our web site at: www.earlyliteracy.cc
For a free color catalog describing Weekly Reader® Early Learning Library's
list of high-quality books, call 1-877-445-5824 (USA) or 1-800-387-3178 (Canada).
Weekly Reader® Early Learning Library's fax: (414) 336-0164.

**Library of Congress Cataloging-in-Publication Data**

Macken, JoAnn Early, 1953-
    Parakeets / by JoAnn Early Macken.
       p. cm. — (Let's read about pets)
    Summary: A simple introduction to parakeets and how to care for them.
    Includes bibliographical references and index.
    ISBN 0-8368-3800-9 (lib. bdg.)
    ISBN 0-8368-3847-5 (softcover)
    1. Parrots—Juvenile literature. [1. Parakeets. 2. Pets.] I. Title.
SF473.P3M24   2003
636.6'864—dc21
                               2003045099

First published in 2004 by
**Weekly Reader® Early Learning Library**
330 West Olive Street, Suite 100
Milwaukee, WI 53212 USA

Editorial: JoAnn Early Macken
Art direction: Tammy Gruenewald
Page layout: Katherine A. Goedheer

Printed in the United States of America

1 2 3 4 5 6 7 8 9 07 06 05 04 03

## Note to Educators and Parents

Reading is such an exciting adventure for young children! They are beginning to integrate their oral language skills with written language. To encourage children along the path to early literacy, books must be colorful, engaging, and interesting; they should invite the young reader to explore both the print and the pictures.

*Let's Read About Pets* is a new series designed to help children learn about the joys and responsibilities of keeping a pet. In each book, young readers will learn interesting facts about the featured animal and how to care for it.

Each book is specially designed to support the young reader in the reading process. The familiar topics are appealing to young children and invite them to read — and re-read — again and again. The full-color photographs and enhanced text further support the student during the reading process.

In addition to serving as wonderful picture books in schools, libraries, homes, and other places where children learn to love reading, these books are specifically intended to be read within an instructional guided reading group. This small group setting allows beginning readers to work with a fluent adult model as they make meaning from the text. After children develop fluency with the text and content, the book can be read independently. Children and adults alike will find these books supportive, engaging, and fun!

— Susan Nations, M.Ed., author, literacy coach, and consultant in literacy development

Parakeets may have blue, white, green, or yellow feathers.  Some parakeets have patches or bands of color.

Parakeets lose
their feathers, or
molt, at least once
a year.  Then new
feathers grow in.

Parakeets can see very well.  They have eyes on the sides of their heads.  This one is looking at you!

A parakeet has a curved **beak**.  It uses its beak to crack open seeds, clean its feathers, and climb.

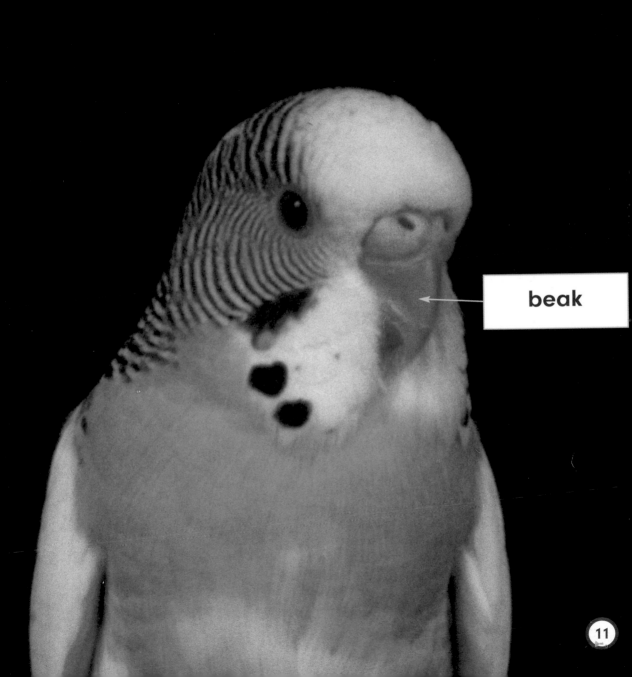

beak

Parakeets eat **seeds** and fresh fruit and vegetables. They also need water to drink.

seeds

Parakeets climb on perches and ladders. They swing on swings. They play with balls and rings.

A parakeet may perch on your finger. It may splash in a birdbath or bowl of water.

A parakeet should fly for a half hour each day. Make sure your house is safe before you open the cage.

19

Parakeets can learn to talk like people. Say a word over and over. Your bird may say it back!

## Glossary

**bands** — stripes

**patches** — areas that are different from other areas around them

**perch** — to land and rest on something; also, a place where a bird rests

# For More Information

**Fiction Books**

Davis, Patricia Anne.  *Brian's Bird*.
   Morton Grove, Ill.: Albert Whitman, 2000.

Jonas, Ann.  *Bird Talk*.  New York:
   Greenwillow Books, 1999.

**Nonfiction Books**

Frost, Helen.  *Birds*.  Mankato, Minn.:
   Capstone Press, 2001.

Stewart, Melissa.  *Small Birds*.  New York:
   Benchmark Books, 2003.

**Web Sites**

**Parakeets**

www.exotictropicals.com/encyclo/birds/parakeets/
parakeets.htm

Parakeet information and photos from Animal World

# Index

## About the Author

**JoAnn Early Macken** is the author of two rhyming picture books, *Sing-Along Song* and *Cats on Judy*, and three other series of nonfiction books. She teaches children to write poetry, and her poems have appeared in several children's magazines. A graduate of the M.F.A. in Writing for Children and Young Adults program at Vermont College, she lives in Wisconsin with her husband and their two sons.